Too Much of a Good Thing

In the land of Scarcity

Breeds Contempt

By

Paul Richmond

Published by Human Error Publishing
Paul Richmond
www.humanerrorpublishing.com
paul@humanerrorpublishing.com

P O Box 838
Greenfield, MA 01302

ISBN:978-09833344-1-5

First Edition
Printed in the United States of America

Previous Releases by Human Error Publishing

No Guarantee's Adjust & Continue
2007
ISBN:978-06151-4136-7

Ready Or Not ......Living in the Break Down Lane
2009
ISBN:9780983334408

Front and Back Cover: Pablo

Too much of a good thing

arrived in an over night express package. A product that promised to deliver the kind of sexual pleasure that had previously only been enjoyed by those who didn't believe in sin. Who saw no reason to deny themselves the enjoyment of pleasure. In the past there were reports that some had died at a young age from a sexual disease. But now, one could enjoy the forbidden pleasures in the safety of their own hands, without the fear of death.

The land of scarcity

has been created for the majority. Along with it an anxiousness that fights for individual rather than a collective or community effort. With the majority having few resources to obtain even the necessities, a small percentage buy products of desire. While the rest dream, look into store windows and fight over the crumbs.

Breeds Contempt

It seems a mystery as to what breeds contempt. What will move people to fight back. Is it having no water to drink? Having land that can't grow food? Having no breathable air? Being forced to live in the streets?

It seems the only way to get a reaction is to offer the latest gadget, with a limited number to go around so everyone won't get one.

Contents

On Her Grave Stone

She loved many

And fought with all

Honey Are You Relaxing

The sun was out
There was a warm breeze
Caressing still cold skin from the north

There was a comfortable chair
Out on the balcony
That he was sitting in
Not comfortably yet

Two weeks to relax
In paradise

A very small lizard
Jumps on to the floor
Disappears quickly
Like it hadn't even been there

A second lizard walked out
A little bigger
Disappears quickly

The third lizard was even larger
He was admiring
Each of these little lizards
He felt so much bigger

The next thought that occurred to him
Based on logic
The three lizards had progressively
Gotten larger
And now being fueled by a vacation party diet
He saw

The next lizard
Being the size of a very large dog
As soon as it pounced
It knocked over the table
And was moving towards him
It was obvious
The lizard wasn't coming towards him
To be petted
He jumps to the railing
With no options
But jumping the two stores

From the other room
His honey asks
Are you relaxing?

A Limber Nut

A limber nut
I never heard of it

Up until the 1930s
This tree grew everywhere
Creating a Limber nut
Limber nuts were plentiful
The birds, the squirrels, the bears
The Indians, the settlers
All ate them

They are now gone
The trees are still around
But they produce no nuts
Things change
Eating habits had to change
In order to survive
The bears haven't adapted so well
There aren't as many bears
The dry season is here early
There are fires
The bears come looking for food
There is little for the Indians that are left
The settlers eat food from somewhere else

The Limber nut trees are still around
But they produce no
Limber nuts
Unlike the human race
That produces nuts everyday

Keeping To The Agenda

Just before
The meeting is to begin
Someone rushes into the room
With last minute changes
To the agenda

Someone else
Leaps to their feet
Yelling
Arguing
That this is not allowed

The Agenda was decided
Days, weeks, months ago

Things have changed
Things are always changing

People argue about it
A motion is made
That we accept change

It's agreed
There is anger
That it didn't happen as planned

A motion is made
That we move on

So that we can keep to the agenda

I Need To Go Home

A light comes into the dark hallway
From a doorway at the end of the hallway
Slightly open
One could hear screams
These were not screams of joy and pleasure
These were screams of fists pounding
With the intent of killing

As the Artist in residence
I was told there are some kids
Who are difficult to work with
I said I wanted to work with them all

I tried to give each of them
Their moment
When I was really there for them
Listening

They were learning to juggle

After a few weeks
The administration
Wanted me to work with the difficult kids
That they talk to me
The administration start asking me
See what you can do
Since you can talk to them
To get them to fit in better

Since I never fit in
I didn't have much to say on that topic

On one of the days
I found myself walking into a classroom
And immediately running to the aid of a teacher
Trying to stop one of the students
From throwing his desk through a window

We physically brought him
Into another room
I was then alone with him
The teacher went to report it
Get help, and go back to her classroom

I sat there looking at him
In silence
I could tell he was expecting
Me to be yelling at him
I asked what was going on?
The young boy said
His father had tried to kill his mother
The father was sent to prison

I acknowledged the fear and anger
One could have
He just looked at me

I asked
What did you hope to accomplish
by throwing your desk through the window?
The boy said
His father was getting out of prison today
And his mother was home alone
The father had said he would kill his mother

I asked did he tell his teacher

He said he asked to go home
When he realized
What his mother had said to him
As he walked out the door

"Your father gets out of prison today
I love you"

I asked what happened when you asked
To go home
He said the teacher had asked
If he wasn't feeling good
He had answered that he felt fine
Then didn't say anything else
She had asked him to sit down

The young boy said
I need to go home

Knowing When To Leave

She said
Why do you have your hand in my blouse?
He said
He was trying to feel her heart beat
She said my heart is on the other side
He said
I am always getting my rights and lefts mixed up

She thought
He gets more than just his rights and lefts
Mixed up
There are Red Flags waving everywhere
She knew
That this was the time
To leave

Help Make Facebook Better For Him

I got an email from Greg's email list
That says
Everyone who is friends with Greg Bechle
He wants to have a party
He has just found out
He has 2 days to 2 weeks to live

It was two weeks
He had a spiritual practice
He was given the name
Greg Shin Do Bechle

5 Months later
His family
Hasn't taken down his Facebook page
There has been no activity

He's dead
He's not gaining any new friends
So here I am
Looking at my Facebook page
And on the right
Where it says Suggestions
There's Greg
And it says
Help make Facebook better for him
Some how I want to tell someone
He's dead
I am not sure he cares about Facebook
And what I wish I could do is have him be alive
I click on him
Just to see what is there

People writing that they miss him
Like he's going to see it
Hopefully he knew we cared
Click back to the action
When I come back
He is gone from my suggestions
He is gone
Physically for sure
I thought I'd write something

Love Thy Self

There are many ways to make this happen

Some go to workshops
Others read books
Some come to it
On their own

Others are sold a bag of goods
Some are dazzled by all the shiny packages
All the products that guarantee
That by having them
You are loving thy self

Others find themselves
Naked
Rubbing oil all over their bodies
Howling at the moon
Wanting to rub themselves on
Anyone who would allow them to

What did you say?
I did wrong
Love thy self
You made a mistake
I did wrong

Sometimes you have to tell the truth
To your self
Love thy self
I did wrong
Make some changes
Love thy self

Turtle In The Road

Raining
Raining
Raining….
So much rain
That, trees are crashing to the ground
Saturated
Heavy with water
They fall pulling out their roots
Just like the ice storms
Only a few months ago

I am driving along
Amazed at how many trees
Are leaning over
Or crashed on the ground

Taking in
How wet
Everything is
I see a turtle in the road
I drive over him, missing him
I tell myself to stop
Pick the turtle up and get
Him or her
To the other side of the road
So it doesn't get squashed

I tell myself it's the thing to do
If I am going to make the world
A better place
We all need to take the time
I tell myself if I was to take time

To pick up every freaking turtle
I would never get anywhere
I would be late for work

Except that doesn't matter
I don't have any work
I am unemployed
So I have the time to stop
I have been driving along
Trying to convince myself
Finally I say I need to do this
To prove to myself that I really care
That my actions do made a difference
So I turn around
I am driving back
Here comes a really big truck
I tell myself
I am going to witness
The consequences of not acting immediately
I could have stopped immediately
Picked this turtle up and it would be safe

Now
Here comes this huge truck

The truck misses the turtle
I see the turtle looking around
Like what the hell is going on
I walk over and realize
I am going to pick up this turtle
I suddenly flash
It is going to take off my finger
It's a snapping turtle
It turns on me and starts to grow

Chases me back to my car
Actually it was a decoy turtle
For the big turtle in the woods
Who is tipping over my car
We are talking Friday night horror movies

I finally snap out of it and reach down
Carefully pick up the turtle
It starts moving in my hand
I wasn't expecting this
And drop the turtle
It hits the ground
I am not sure if I broke a leg
Or dented his skull
I looked around
Hoping no one had seen this display
Pulling myself together
I pick up the turtle
And take it to the other side
The turtle was hiding in its shell
I thought I heard cursing
I never saw the turtle come out

I then heard on the radio
That some kid
Had died
They were warning parents
That if they buy turtles for pets
They have to make sure their children
Don't suck on them
Some kid had one in his mouth
Got some kind of bacteria infection
Died

What I learned that day
Was another reminder
To listen to myself
To act on my feelings of kindness
To take the time for acts of kindness
That when picking up live beings
They will move
And I need to not drop them
Or learn first aid
And
Don't suck on turtles

There Are Bodies In The Streets On Mondays

I walked into a store
I said do you realize
That there are bodies lying out in the street

They asked me what day it was
I said it was Monday

They said Yes
There are always bodies
Laying out in the streets on Mondays
I said what do you mean
There are always
Bodies in the streets on Mondays

They said
Over the weekend people get stressed out
Facing a new week
With No jobs
More debt
Nothing has changed
Tension is high
Fighting all weekend

There are bodies in the streets on Mondays

The politicians are arguing
A vote is being called
The proposal is to eliminate weekends

Some are trying to add an amendment
Blaming violence on TV
Others see the complaint about the bodies

As a distraction
From the real business at hand
Giving more tax cuts to the rich

When I ask others what can we do?
To stop seeing the bodies
In the streets on Mondays
Someone suggests
Stop walking the streets on Mondays

Recognizing this historical manifestation
I knew we would soon
Not be walking the streets on Tuesday

There are things that can be done
To stop having bodies in the streets

One Hopes Not

There is the fear of death
There is the reality of death
The fear of being brutalized
The stories of couples being torn apart
Sexually abused in front of each other
The helplessness to stop it
The force of power and hatred
The fear that this will happen
In what seems it's random way
Striking here

One hopes not

I Am Not Your Baby

She answered the phone
He said Baby I miss ya
She said I don't think so
He said Baby I love ya
She said I don't believe ya
He said Baby I am really trying
She said
You'er not trying hard enough
He said Baby
You know how much I care
For you
She said I don't know
He said Baby
Why are you putting me off like this
She said
You've got the wrong number
I am not your Baby

Our Eyes Meet

Our eyes meet
We didn't know each other

Our eyes meet
There was no looking away
Everything was calm

Our eyes meet
We smiled
It felt like we knew each other
We joked
We laughed
It was uncomplicated

No one got hurt
It was just a moment
Of enjoying each other

Our eyes meet
It felt good

I awoke from sleep
And my dream
Was hopeful
What might happen today?
First
I need to leave my solitude
For our eyes to meet

Spider Philosophy

I was standing in the shower
Asking myself
What kind of day would this be?

I looked into the tub
And noticed a Spider
The Spider was obviously
Trapped
In the tub

I watched it
Trying to climb up the wall of the tub
It would get so far
And slide down
It did this a couple of times
I thought
Life can be such a bitch
You try really hard
To only slide back down

I noticed the spider
Moving around
Trying different places
That was depressing

Then again what else is one suppose to do?
The spider wanted out
The spider was smart enough
To not try
In the same place over and over again

Here I was looking in from above

Seeing the large tub
With the spider on one end
It was obvious
The spider was trapped
The same thing would happen
All the away around
The spider would climb up a certain distance
And slide back down
As I looked over
It slide down one more time
I got a yogurt container
As it was climbing up again
I got under it

It knew I was there
With the intent of getting it into the container
The spider tried some fast moves
I thought
Oh great
I am going to get bit now
Trying to help this spider
Then it was in the container
I walked it outside
Wondering what the spider
Would do on being dumped out
I turned the container over
Waiting to see it on the ground
Watch it realize it was free

Nothing
Looked inside
Figured it was stuck inside
The container was empty
There was no spider

Not sure when it got out
As I walked from the bathroom to the porch

It was just a lesson in spider philosophy
You give it all you got
You keep trying
No matter how many times you fall
You get up and try again
And Yes

The cosmos
Something bigger helps
Steps in and lifts you out
Of the times
That we're sliding down and going nowhere
And in the end
It is still a mystery
Where we are going

Hunky-Dory

Our main character
Was a little slow
In his awareness
Of what was going on around him
He thought of himself as a sensitive guy

It occurred one day to our main character
That he and his wife were eating a lot of carrots

He had heard that carrots were good for him
His wife prepared carrots for every meal
He began to like carrots
He looked forward to the carrots
As the days turned into weeks

Our main character
Who is always listening for the pulse
Recognized a familiar snapping sound
Coming from the other room
Over the last few weeks
He had accepted this sound
As just part of the background ambiance
Never wondering what it was
Today he decided
He'd investigate

He found his wife
Putting a carrot
Into her vagina
Then without using her hands
She would break them
With a snapping sound

Being the sensitive guy
He then noticed
He lost his sex drive
And
He lost his taste for carrots
And
It occurred to him
Maybe everything isn't
Hunky-Dory

Sand Runs Out

(On Dec. 6th 2009 30 poets read for 3 minutes each, a sand timer was used to keep time.)

The sand is running
I have 3 minutes of sand
I only get 3 minutes
Lets complain about only having 3 minutes
And waste time complaining

What can be said in 3 minutes?
I hate feeling rushed
When you rush
You fumble
You forget things to say
Now I have wasted time talking about that

What's there to talk about?
What needs to be talked about?

Oh just get to the point
Whatever the point is

Here it is

We are at war
What is the real reason?

After 6 years
What has been accomplished?
Hundreds of Billions of dollars
Exploded
Another 30 billion being asked for

The real cost is devastating
How many more sons and daughters?
Who's taking care of the Vets that make it home?

We don't' have money for libraries
Schools
Health Care
Unemployment rising
We make nothing we need

Where's our reliable green infrastructures

Instead
A few get rich

Everyone else fights over
The crumbs
Low paying jobs that produce useless garbage

And how many different ways
Does it need to be said?
Until there is a change
Spoken Words
Some try to capture them
Repeat them
Put them on posters
On T shirts
Create slogans
Chant them
What will make a change?

The sand is running

Lets talk about

The holidays

Happy Holidays
What kind of memories do you have?

Were they drunken?
Fights with crying

Or was it warm and cuddly?
With gifts and food
And hugs and kiss
And Train sets to play with

Or was it both
Just to make it confusing

And lets not forget
What's the score and whose team is winning?
Do you hear the crowds cheering?

While our cities crumble
The homeless gaining numbers
Why can't we provide basic needs?

How many people can the earth support?
Live simply

And oh man
Stop talking so fast and asking all these questions
Because I am feeling an urgency
I am feeling stressed out

And I am trying to relax
I am on holiday

With no money
There's no relaxing
I am told to buy things
I am told if I don't buy things
The whole thing will go down

Let me just be clear

I don't like what is going on

I want there to be a change

Words have power

Take 3 minutes

Feel the power

I've got time for silence

And in the silence

One can find answers

There has always been a fight

All we need to do is not cooperate

Is it really that simple?
Just not cooperating
Without us it falls apart
We make it happen

Lets work cooperatively

To fulfill basic needs

Knock Knock
Who's there?
3
3 who
3 minutes
Sand Runs Out

It Was Delicious

I walked into the bar
Walked over to a table
She was sitting by herself
When I approached
She said
Hi Handsome
I said Hi Delicious
She said have a seat
It was a booth
I sat next to her
That way
I could
Have my hand
Under the table
Holding her hand
Squeezing her thigh

She said do you want to order
I said yes
She asked what did I want to order
I said
I want you
She smiled
Squeezed my thigh

We meet like this once a month
We have been together for years

We didn't talk about bills
We didn't' talk about who didn't do what
We didn't' talk about our disappointments
We looked into each other's eyes

I asked her
If she wanted to come home with me

She hesitated

Just to pull my   chain

Then she said
Lets go to my place

We went home

It was delicious

I Had An Itch

She sat in a chair
With very short shorts
Showing a lot of leg
She sat with her legs on another chair
She kept caressing her thigh

She slipped her hand
Into her tight shorts

She kept reaching in
As if she had an itch

I wondered
What it would be like to scratch it
I didn't linger there too long
Me 60
Her 25
It was her itch
And right now she was scratching it
We continued our talk
About college
Travel
Being young and living your life

After our talk
I did notice
I had an itch

A Prompt

Use these words

Rapture
Slippery
Gastronomy
Pomegranate
Superlative
Swamp Meat
Ass
Ancient
Light
Inspiration

Potluck
I was invited to a potluck
Of people I didn't know
Who regularly gather to share food
I was told the theme was Ancient
I wanted to impress
I wanted to fill my guest with rapture
To impress them
With my knowledge of Gastronomy
I am not sure if my choice of Swamp Meat
Was the best choice
Why I didn't realize
That some don't like their food slippery
I thought I was being clever
By making a pomegranate sauce
That I thought would inspire
Instead I was put out on my ass
Told never to return
Without even a superlative

Premenstrual

She cries

She remembers that it is her son's birthday soon
She starts crying

She asks a question
He makes a joke
It is missed
Taken seriously
Has to be explained
They are suddenly in an argument
He asks about something
She feels repeatedly
That she has given the answer to before
He has forgotten
He asks again
She says he never listens
Another argument starts

He asks if she is premenstrual
She says these arguments
Have nothing to do with her being premenstrual
And that starts an argument

He tells himself
He needs to mark her cycle
In his calendar
Then again
When he's paying attentions
He doesn't need a calendar
He knows
When she is
Premenstrual

When The Light Turned Red

He talked of the revolution
In Brazil
How the rich watched it from up in their penthouses
From up on the hill
With cameras that zoomed down into the action
The rich were upset
For the sound was not working
All they could do was watch silent screens
He watched the tanks roar through the streets
He laughed
As he watched the tanks
Approach intersections
Where they stopped
When the light turned red

Living Communally
The Meetings That Never End # 4,032

As the camera zooms in
Nothing has been decided
Besides
The known facts
The stove devours electric
The fridge
Warms things up
The dogs shit all over the house
No fuel for the winter
Chimney needs to be fixed

What gets decided
Paul makes calls to fix chimney
Four o'clock pick up new stove and fridge
Shashana
Calling for fire Insurance
Schedule another meeting

The Sun Was In Her Eyes

Outside the bookstore
I walked up to her
She lowered her head

I thought this isn't a good sign

She just lowered her Head
This meant no eye contact
It seemed a clear image
Of don't talk to me

On the train, the other day
I saw this woman stand up
There was a wildness about her

I guy stood up
And moves towards her
Already, with smile and rap
She kept her gaze
Out of his reach
He saw no opening
He could of just started talking
He didn't
Her fixed gaze, away from him
Silenced him
She gave no opening

He stood back
Just looking at her
Running his feelings
That he wasn't worth
Her glaze

The doors opened to the train
And she walked out
She was going somewhere
And was not going to be stopped

Back at the bookstore
I asked why she put her head down
Kept her gaze from my direction
She said

The sun was in her eyes

Alphabet Relationships

These stories are about
Relationships among people
The names of people are letters
So the sex is not obvious
It doesn't' matter what sex you are
We are all capable of treating each other
Either very beautifully or ugly
These stories are short glimpses into relationships

JKLM

K said to L
I saw you next to M
L said
That's just the way it is
K said
I don't want you next to M
L said
Why don't you snuggle up to J
K said
I want to snuggle up to M
K said
I don't want you next to M
L said
It's just the way it is
JKLM

U Asked A Question
T Left Never To Return

T was ripping up U's old love letters
Once T had ripped up the letters
The photo albums were brought out
Each picture removed
Ripped into small pieces
As the pile grew
U searched for clues in the tiny little pieces
The photo albums were now empty
They themselves destroyed
Beyond recognition
Now those special gifts
That represented a moment
A key to a door of memories
All boiled down to some trinket
That T was now
Crushing
Grinding
Pounding
Into dust

There was silence
As U and T
Sat in the dust filled room
T finally looked up
U asked
Are you mad at me?

What About Us

W and P
Were standing
In an intersection
Car horns were Blaring
People were screaming
Move out of the way
Get out of the street

W and P were having words
With each other
In the middle of the intersection
The light had changed
There they stood

It might seem like
An unlikely place
It all happened so suddenly
As they held hands
Crossing the intersection diagonally

As they walked
P felt the urge to tell W

P turned towards W
And to W's smiling face
Said
I am in love with Z

W felt the earth give way
There was no intersection,
No honking horns
No yelling people

Only the urgent need
To ask
What does that mean?
What about us?

A Matter Of Trust And Integrity

I walked into the house

I said
Hi Honey
She said
You no good Son of Bitch
You broke your promise
You lied
You told me you wouldn't

How could you do this to me?
What about us?
Can't you keep you pants on?
She said, how can I trust you?
If you say one thing and do another

I had promised her
I would tell her
Any time I was going to drop my draws

I admitted
I had dropped my draws

To moon our politicians
Who stand before us
As they pretend to tell the truth

She saw it on TV

She finally calmed down
When she found the note
I had left

Saying
I'd had enough

I was going to Moon the liars
I had tried to let her know
She thanked me for the note
But
She still didn't trust me

By Day We Are Singular And Often Lonely
(A line from Denise Levertov)

By Day we are singular and often lonely
Even though we live and walk among millions
Eyes that meet and eyes that don't
Exchanges of information
Socially accepted ways of greeting
Business etiquette to relationships
Religious ceremonies void of any spirit
People, people everywhere
Doesn't change that
We are singular and often lonely

The Army Of Ants, Are On The Move

They're coming
They're coming
The cry is heard
There are rumors that there are millions
Others say there are too many to count

Some say put baking soda around the cracks
Others are religious about cleaning up the crumbs
My mother boiled water
And poured it on the black moving carpet
As it moves towards our house

Others know there is no defense
The army of ants
Are on the move
One can only hope they move on by

To See What Is On The Other Side

Is it in the late night?
That the poet finds their words
The Artist materializes

Is it after a long night of drinking?
Or doing drugs?
Is it always the one who is wild?
Takes everything to extremes
Is a passionate lover
Every time
For this may be their last
Many die young

Why is it rarely the ones dressed in suits
The ones who follow orders
Is it the every day job?
Doing the same thing every day
Having to have everything in it's place
That doesn't allow one
To cross the line
To see what is on the other side

The Lost Cafe

I didn't have much money
So I order the cheapest items on the menu
I ordered a kids portion of French toast
I was brought a pile of Blueberry pancakes
With ice cream on the side
I ordered a small side dish
Of home fries
I received a plate
Of grilled steak, sausages, and bacon
Which the waitress said
Came with the large plate of home fires
I ordered a small orange juice
I was given a large pitcher
I said I'd like some coffee
And the pot was brought over
I ask the waitress what was going on
She said this is how it is here
I said wow
I want to live here
Just then
My alarm clock woke me

In the cold kitchen
I found I was out of eggs
The milk was sour
The mice had gotten into the cereal
Looking out the window
I couldn't see the corner store
The snow was a white curtain with a howling wind
That wouldn't have stopped me

But

My wallet was empty
I went back to bed
I lay there
Closing my eyes
Tightly
Knowing
I wasn't going to find that cafe

I Was Hesitant About The Rest Of My Day

After ordering
2 eggs over easy
Wheat toast and orange juice

I received 2 eggs broken against the wall

Burnt white toast soggy with butter

Warm vinegar
Called orange juice

At the cash register
The Waitress
Said have a good day

I was hesitant about the rest of my day

I Know What I Want

I was handed a menu
And asked what do I want to order

I said I wanted the waitress
More then I wanted the breakfast

I was told the waitress wasn't on the menu

I explained

I don't order from menus
I know what I want

I Had To Have Seconds

Instead of bringing the orange juice
She let her gown drop to the floor
And laid herself on the table

When I was asked why I was late for work

I said that my breakfast was so good
I had to have seconds

She Said Welcome To My World

He said that he was thinking
She said she knew he was thinking
She wanted to hear what he was feeling

He was thinking about the dream he was sold
Of being with the goddess
The model
The super model

Yes there are contests
Women are rated
Who is a 10

A woman who was told
She was a 1.8
Loved rejecting men in bars
During the last call
When everyone looked like a 10

Did he feel respectable for settling for a 5.9?
All one had to do is
Become rich
Have power
Be higher up on the ladder
Then you had a chance of getting closer to a 10

Those who possessed 10's are disappointed
When an 11 is found
Then the battle is on for the 11

What does that have to do with
Lumps in the breast

Tumors on the cervix
Legs blown off by land minds
Being forced into prostitution

And while some are being dressed up
In negligee
So many are dying
From abuse
Being raped
Forced into slavery

Look someone found a 12

He said he was thinking
When would we learn to love?
And
He was feeling a little numb
She said welcome to my world

He Always Changes The Subject

She said if you keep lying
I don't know who you are
And that mean's
I can't love you

This made him pause for a moment

Since he didn't know what it meant to be in love
Since he had been lying to himself
He couldn't be loved
Since he couldn't find himself

After a long silence
She said well, what do you have to say
About the lying?
He looked her straight in the eyes
And said
I prefer sitting up to lying down

I Was Looking For Love

I was looking for love,
Until someone turned off the lights,
I stumbled through the dark,
Until I found out
How to turn on the lights myself
And found
The love that was always there

Won't Remember My Name

She said you don't remember my name
Do You?
He said Oh my honey pie
Baby you are my delight
She said
You say that to all the women
He said ohhh gorgeous
I am here for you
She said
You're here now
But you won't remember my name

Broccoli

She would break off
Individual broccoli heads
And twilled them between her fingers
While she looked at me
And licked her lips
I remembered this when being asked
When did my obsession start with broccoli?

Commissioned Poem

"Something about the juxtaposition of the modern
In the historic. The blending of internet and brick and
mortar....but funny." By BG

I was asked to write
A poem
That would be about 5 minutes
The communications happen with email
Something unknown 25 years ago
It wasn't face to face
It wasn't by a letter
Or by phone
It was through an email
Over the internet

Would I like to write a poem?
I said what kind of poem?
Is there a theme?
And an email came back
For the Arts Block

Something about the juxtaposition of the modern
In the historic
The blending of internet and brick and mortar
But funny

Of course this drove me into an
Inspirational frenzy
Being an Artist
Since I was being offered some cash

I said of course

I had already thought of thousands of things
Nothing related to this
But that is part of the creative process

Let's start with the first aspect
The cash
And being an Artist
Which brought on a smile
It doesn't make it funny for the audience
Then again
If the artist isn't happy
Then the art usually isn't happy either

Historically
As artists
We have always had to find
Patrons
Who like our art
Or us
And are willing to pay for it

My mother thought it was enough
To put it on the refrigerator door

But after a while
It lost it's reinforcement

At school getting those little stickers
Remembering my Art Teacher saying
Look class Paul's drawing almost looks like a dog
I was going to inform the teacher it was a bird

But I wanted the sticker
And leaned early on

To never interpret art for others
And kept my mouth shut

This started me down the path of being an Artist
Creatively paying the rent
For studios
Which are brick and mortar

Artists look for abandoned buildings or
Slum landlords who live in other states or
A Patron with a building

These studios are usually where Artists live
By throwing down a mattress
Calling this place their studio
When really it is their apartment
Artist's try to elevate
These crash pads to something lofty
Where they attempt to create art

Usually when someone comes to these hovels
And sees the mattress on the floor
The dirty dishes, the rats and cockroaches
The Artist explains the rats are pets

And they are training the cockroaches to do tricks
These and other delusions
Has the artists believing
That in case their art doesn't sell
They have a back up career
Of being an animal trainer

The problem is, once all the artists move
Into all the abandoned buildings

Coffee shops spring up everywhere
In brick and mortar
Then little sandwich shops

Salvation Army and thrift stores
Where Artist buy their clothes and props

This suddenly transforms sections of town
Into hip places to be
With people sitting around in cafes
The empty storefronts
Again Brick + Mortar
Become galleries where Artists bring their work
People start arriving
Asking what is this stuff?
What does it mean?
The honest artist has learned to ask
What do you think, feel it is?
And when they say that it expresses their deepest
Emotions from their soul
The artist learns to nod
For this is a canvas that was on the floor
When the Artist was painting their walls
During a break up
So the paint splatter
Was emotional

The canvas was cut up and framed
The paintings sell
Then the Artist is trapped

Has been defined
And is forced to keep producing this type of art
When really they wanted to be a singer

Except any time they did that
The police were called
Since someone thought there was
Abuse going on
In the studio down the hall

Artist have it tougher now
It's hip to want to fix up these abandoned places

Which is making for less and less places
For any artist to live
I mean create
And the coffee suddenly goes up from 35 cents
To $4.00 for a tall
So the Artist can't really live there

So all the artists leave
Then the artists that paint by numbers move in
The situation changes

By the way Brick + Mortar in Greenfield
We are referring to an International Video Festival

Historically I didn't grow up with videos, DVD's, etc
I had 3 channels to choose from in Black and White
And I was told there was an educational channel
Which when I realized there were no King Kong movies
Or Abbot and Costello, or the 3 Stooges
I never watched it

Growing up I could only talk on the phone
For very short periods of time
Which kept me always longing
For my crushes at school

Now the youth can call anywhere in the world
Talk as much as they want

Text, watch videos, make videos etc
On
Their phones

My friend's 12 year old
Already has 3 books published online
Thousands of fans
A youtube channel with all the movies
They directed and produced
Their blog is thousands of words long

I finally posted a poem
Was happy
To accept another friend request on facebook
Was feeling loved
I had finally reached 23 friends
With others having thousands of pictures
That they post daily
I am still reading the manual

But back to being an artist and today's gallery
It is not on the streets or abandoned buildings
No your Gallery, is no longer brick and mortar
Now an artist must have a web page
The internet
Where one has ones gallery
Where it looks fancy and professional
So now an artist must find an alley way
Near a cyber cafe
To put their refrigerator box they call home
But no one knows this

Since the web site looks professional
Everything has been photoshoped
Including their art
In the hopes to make it look better
Like removing the coffee stains on the canvas

There is one problem with this
You have to make web sites
You need money in order to have a web site
To have a computer and the software to do this
Reading more manuals

Trying to understand how 0's and 1's
Allows you to have a picture of a paint brush
That goes across the top of the page
To give your site something special
Since you are a painter like no other
You can't just say you are a painter
The page has to be dynamic

Then there is the new market place
Where you hang with people
You don't know
Who you call your friends
Called social networking
Where you each give lip service
To each other's creations
But really everyone is waiting for sales
What really hurts
Is to see your master pieces on ebay
Being sold for the materials you used
Being a conscious artist
You know the importance of recycling
You just wish it was with someone else's work

So the question is what has changed

What has gone on historically to the present

How has this blending
Of the internet and brick & mortar
Made things better for Artists
Now instead of confiding in one friend
The artists can express their angst
About survival, share their neuroses
Complain about their poverty
To hundreds if not thousands of people
With one click of the mouse

How this will effect the kind of art
That is created now
Compared to art created long ago
We will all intrepret for ourselves
One thing is for sure
It still is a struggle

I am really grateful that there is some cash
And there is some free food and coffee
And the chance to present this work
Which I got off an internet site called
Creative talks for Artist to give at luncheons
I made copies
So when you go home
You can put it on your refrigerator

Everyone Out Of The Pool

Being a landlord
He said one time he went to collect the rent
They said they didn't have it
He said he would have to throw them out
They were many months behind
As he turned
He was stabbed in the back with a syringe

He was a landlord of an apartment complex
Another time he said he got a complaint about water I
Leaking
From the ceiling

In the living room
All the apartments were the same
There was a living room above
There shouldn't be any water leaking from there
Thought the person was making it up
He went into the apartment

Sure enough water was dripping down from the ceiling
He knocked on the door of the apartment above
When they opened the door
What he saw was two couches
One full of adults sitting drinking beer
Laughing
On the other couch
Were the kids
Using the couch as a diving board
To jump into the pool they had put into the living room
It was full of water
With the help of the police and fire department
The tenants were informed
Everyone out of the Pool

74

It Must Be All That Practicing

I noticed that you had your hand in my pants
You weren't doing anything with your hand
You just had it in my pants
When asked why you had your hand in my pants
You said you were practicing
Self restraint
You've always accused me
Of encouraging you to abandon
The limitations you've set up for yourself
I try and justify
What I am asking for
Is really good for you

I have to admit
You are good at holding to your limits
It must be all that practicing

The Back Table

There was a back table
In a dark corner
There were only a few tables back there
The other tables were empty
They sat not across from each other
But next to each other
With their backs up against the wall
With the table between them and everyone else
The tablecloth hung down low
Giving them a lot of cover
Back there
They squeezed each other
Let their arms and hands
Slide around on each other
As their lips touched
And their tongues talked to each other
And the Music played in the background
It was a hot night

They looked into each others eyes
What conversation there was
Went like this
Wow
This is amazing
I can't believe it
I hope this lasts forever

A few years later
Sitting at that same table
Alone
Waiting for you to arrive
Our anniversary

We come here every anniversary
And smooch up a storm
At the back table

Available

It was passed through word of mouth

He's moved out
Is living with friends
Has gotten his own apartment

Some immediately think of the children
How are they doing with the break up

Other discuss that they knew it was going to happen
Others are saying they don't know why it took so long
Still others had held them up
As the couple who would always be together

He was seen with a younger woman
Some women hated him for it
Some men were jealous
Others were glad to know
Now his X was available

I Want A Change

We sat across from each other in the restaurant
She was sitting facing me

The man she was sitting with
Sat with his back to me
Their table was directly across the small room

I was sitting in a booth
That had a circular table

The woman I was with sat next to me
The conversation in our booth
Was more of a report
An analysis
By my partner
With verbal graphs

Clearing showing
My falling short of expectations
In fact it was being reported
That in some areas
I wasn't even on the chart

I watch the man with his back to me
Gesture as he spoke
I watched her look at me
Look at him
Look at me

I noticed that we were both not talking
A few words here and there

I looked at her
And Him gesturing
And listened to my partner
What she was saying
Seemed to match his gesturing

I thought
Is it possible
We are both getting the same rap
Would it be better
For our partners to be together

As we kept looking
Making eye contact

A strong feeling
Came over me
We should be together

I am just going to get up
Head for the door
I just got this strong feeling
That if one of us made a move for the door
The other would follow

I got up
She watched me get out of the booth
Did I read disappointment?
As I didn't head for the door
I went to the bathroom

When I came back
They were gone
The waiter brought our check

My partner asked

So do you think things can change?
I said
I want a change

I Just Don't Feel Satisfied

Please don't hang up
Calls are taken in the order they are received
If you hang up now you will lose your place
Please continue to hold
The next available assistant will assist you

We appreciate your patience
Please don't hang up
Your call is important to us
If you hang up now you will lose your place
For calls are answered in the order they were received

Hello
Welcome to Satisfaction Guaranteed incorporated
Please listen closely
For our menu items are always changing
In the hope to serve you better
Press 1 for Mail in rebates
Press 2 if it's Tuesday
Press 3 if you are late
Press 4 for more options

Press 10 to cut the Military Budget
Press 11 to tax the corporations
Press 12 to tax the rich
Press 13 to make a change

Press 38 for hysterectomy
Press 39 for a colonoscopy
Press 40 for hair removal
Press 41 for more options

Press 69 for hints of why you called
Press 97 if you are dissatisfied

97

Hello, I am your customer satisfaction specialist
I am here to solve your problems
Fix what has been broken
Return what needs to be returned
Make sure what you thought you were getting
You get

Can I have your customer number please?

I don't' have a customer number

Well sir
In order for me to do my job
I need a customer number

But that's my problem
I don't want a number

Sir, we all have numbers

Check the bottom of the box
Look on the upper left hand corner of your invoice

I am sorry I don't have any of those things

If you give me your credit card number
I can try and trace it to your order
I didn't use a credit card

How about your check number and bank name

I just don't feel satisfied

I am sure you don't sir
As soon as I get the needed information
I can change all that
For I am a customer satisfaction specialist

I was hoping you could help

I can sir
Lets start with what's wrong

I just don't feel satisfied

I understand that sir
Did you receive the wrong color?
Is it the wrong size?
Are their parts missing?

No
Did the software not load?
Is the unit not turning on?

Do you have it plug in?

That's not my problem

Ok sir why don't you tell me what is the problem

I just don't feel satisfied

Would you like to return the item for a refund?

I not suppose to give refunds
But for you sir I would

I don't have an item to return
Sir this is my specialty
This is my job
If I don't do my job I could lose it
So try working with me here
What is wrong?

I told you
I just don't feel satisfied

Sir I can return your money
I can send you a new one
I can extend the contract for free
I can offer free shipping

I am sorry none of that helps

Sir, I am going to transfer you
Hold on

Hello
I am your customer satisfaction specialist
How can I help you?

I just don't feel satisfied

This Is Going To Be A Long Wait

He sits with his arms crossed
He looks frustrated
She keeps talking
She asks questions
That he doesn't answer
Everyone once in a while
He says he doesn't want to talk about it
She doesn't always look at him
He shakes his head
He tries to look off in another direction
She turns towards him and keeps talking
He doesn't answer
His hands stay crossed
She keeps talking
This is in an airport
She gets up
Going off to the bathroom
When she leaves his face relaxes
He has silence
He doesn't smile
He breathes deep
Looking off into the distance

With her still gone
He finally looks at his watch
His hands
Become uncrossed
Rest in his lap

Then a woman next to him
Takes out her cell phone
And starts talking loudly

Has taken out her papers
He turns to look towards her
His hands cross again against his chest
He is breathing heavily again

Then his wife comes back
With a bag of potato chips
There are times he looks like he is going to talk
His mouth open
But he says nothing
She keeps asking questions
He nods his head up and down

Saying something he has said
Many times
Is tired of saying it
He now has two women
Talking on both sides of him
He looks back and forth
More heavy breathing
Arms stay crossed

Suddenly he gets up
To get away
He walks to the screens
Reads the departure info
The plane is delayed
He comes back
She starts talking
He closes his eyes
As if he is trying to sleep
She keeps talking
About this and that
Asking questions he has no answers to

The woman next to him
On the cell phone
Is now yelling

This is going to be a long wait

How I Wanted To Be Taken

When I looked into her eyes
I felt lighter
I felt I was being swept up
And Taken
OHHH
How I wanted to be taken

Later in court listening to her lawyer
I couldn't see her eyes
She was looking the other way
Head down
Blocked by her lawyer
No
I had no regrets

In the drone of the lawyer
Just asking for what is fair
I remember how willingly I went
How I cheered
How my face was plastered with a smile
Looking into her eyes
I felt lighter
I felt swept away
OHHH
How I wanted to be taken

I was then informed by the judge
Just how much I was going to be taken for
I will always remember her
For she had me
Feel lighter
I felt swept away
OHHH How I was taken

Clueless

She walked into the room with her bags

He looked up and said
Sweetie Pie how's my delicious
She looked at him in disbelief
She thought
Will he ever wake up

He said
My love
I look forward to the future

She walked toward the door

He said
My pumpkin
I love your pie

Her eyes now looked to the floor
As if words might be found there
The nagging feeling
Of there must be something to say

He was going on about
The love binding them
Was the strongest glue in the world

She opened the door

And walked out

Years later

As he waited for her to return
A friend asks
How can you be so
Clueless

Smoochie Moochie

Yes Smoochie Moochie
I wondering why I don't have more
Smoochie Moochie
In my life
I decided to go out and look for it
I found others who were interested

With many it was like Lighting striking
Then soon there was the thunder
A devastating storm
It had me question just what was
Smoochie Moochie
And why did I think I needed it

Learn A New Language

Our Main Character was told
If you masturbate
You will go blind

Our Main Character's first thought
Stop immediately

But Our Main Character's Love
For science and the truth

Required daily experiements

Where our Main Character enjoyed researching

This was all scienitificly done

With regularly eye exams

Since there was no evidence that
Blindness was instantanous after Masturbating
Our Main Character was willing to gamble
That the process might take some time
More of a gradual blindness
So why not enjoy
Until you needed glasses

When that happens
Our Main Character thought
The responsible action
Would be to reconsider the options
Stop masturbating
Or go Blind

The choice was easy
Our main character would go back to school
And learn a new language
Braille

Listen To The Trees Talking With The Wind

How's it running?
It's running as smoothly
As riding on a roller coaster
With a few wheels missing

The riders are screaming
We don't know if they are screaming
For Joy

The expressions on their faces
Varies with each face
We will have to wait until the ride ends

I went to talk to the ride attendant
And found no one there
I found no levers or switches
To stop the ride
There were blinking lights
But nothing
That gave a clear way
Of gaining control of the ride

Back to the screaming riders
Are they tourists?
Did they know what they were getting into?
Did they go willingly?
Do they believe?
That this is what one does
Get taken for a ride

Was it luck?
That I got there late

There were still more seats available
I watched as others scrambled for the seats
As the ride moved out of the gate

I walked away
Far enough away
From the screaming riders
So I could hear the birds
Listen to the trees
Talking with the wind

My Best Pieces Are 4 Minutes

(Performed 2010, December reading where
everyone had 3 minutes)

Only having 3 minutes
Is a Problem
All my best pieces are 4 minutes long
Wanting to impress
With my best
I thought of trimming
Down to 3 minutes
Yet as a Writer
It's difficult to take out words

I notice in my 4-minute pieces
Each word was needed
To reach into the audience's Soul
To have a real communication
Causing audience's faces
To become canvases
For the emotions of each word
And when the words were really cooking
There were ooowww sounds
And in some of those 4 minute pieces
I counted 22 ooowws
And 15 ahhhhs
There were even some places
Where you heard
Applause
I tried to remember
Where the applause happens
For I wanted to remember those words
The words that cooked

I wanted to repeat them
As many times as possible

Since I don't have 4 minutes
And I couldn't trim to 3 minutes
And now less then 3 minutes
How to say in a poetic way

The earth is being destroyed for profits
The rich are getting richer
The politician are bought off
So many fight for crumbs
Wars are constant
Militarism is our industry
Millions unemployed
Water that is undrinkable
Air unbreathable
Soil that has been drained of its life
Agriculture that is controlled by those that sell seeds
Seeds that grow plants that produce no seeds
All our resources being used to destroy
A sustainable environment
And by the way
The doctor can't see you now
And could you please stop being
Hysterical
You might wake up those around you

An on an on

This can be depressing
A bummer
And doesn't make for a funny poem
Ho Ho Ho

To feel inspired
To write something
In the hopes
To manifest change
With plenty
Of owwws and ahhhs
To be a part of a sharing
For it is with our voices
The truth can be heard
And it can be done
In less then 3 minutes

Previously Published

"It Was Delicious" was published in Silkworm 4
The Annual Review of the Florence Poets Society

"Honey Are You Relaxing", "Knowing When To Leave",
were published in Silkworm 5
The Annual Review of the Florence Poets Society

Commissioned Poem, was a commissioned poem for an
event for the International Brick & Mortar Video Festival
in 2010, presented at the Arts Block in Greenfield, MA

"I Know What I Want", "I Had To Have Seconds" and
"Learn A New Language" were all in the On Line Global
Gallery Show of 2011.

"When The Light Turned Red" - Was given an
Honorable Mention Award at the Austin International
Poetry Festival 2011 by 2005 Texas Poet Laureate Alan
Birkelbach and published in the 2011 Anthology.

Comments

"One thing I really appreciated from your poems was the
acknowledgement, and a fair degree of affirmation, of
our sexuality, as it is." Jeffrey Benson

"You are a poetry god with timing and reverent
irreverence, like if moses, steven wright, lucille ball, tina
fey and george carlin had an orgy." Tommy Twilite